The Modern Gilpin, C the Adventures of John Oldstock: In an Excursion by Steam from London to Rochester Bridge : Containing a Passing Glance at the Principal Places On the Thames and Medway : With Notes

William Cowper

THE

MODERN GILPIN;

OR, THE

Adventures of John Oldstock,

IN AN EXCURSION BY STEAM FROM LONDON TO
ROCHESTER BRIDGE.

CONTAINING

A PASSING GLANCE AT THE PRINCIPAL PLACES
ON THE THAMES AND MEDWAY;

WITH NOTES.

ILLUSTRATED BY AN EMINENT ARTIST.

LONDON:

PRINTED AND PUBLISHED BY J. CROCKER,
5, GARNAULT-PLACE, SPAFIELDS;

SOLD ALSO BY BERGER, HOLYWELL STREET, STRAND; PATTIE, BRYDGES-
STREET, STRAND; PURKESS, OLD COMPTON-STREET, SOHO;
STRANGE, PATERNOSTER-ROW.

And may be had of all Booksellers and Newsmen.

M DCCC XXXVIII.

Entered at Stationers' Hall.

PRICE SIXPENCE.

The Modern Gilpin.

THE

MODERN GILPIN;

OR, THE

Adventures of John Oldstock,

IN AN EXCURSION BY STEAM FROM LONDON TO
ROCHESTER BRIDGE.

CONTAINING

A PASSING GLANCE AT THE PRINCIPAL PLACES
ON THE THAMES AND MEDWAY:

WITH NOTES.

ILLUSTRATED BY AN EMINENT ARTIST.

LONDON:

PRINTED AND PUBLISHED BY J. CROCKER,
5, GARNAULT-PLACE, SPAFIELDS;
SOLD ALSO BY BERGER, HOLYWELL-STREET, STRAND; PATTIE, BRYDGES-
STREET, STRAND; PURKESS, OLD COMPTON-STREET, SOHO;
STRANGE, PATERNOSTER-ROW.
And may be had of all Booksellers and Newsmen.
M DCCC XXXVIII.

ENTERED AT STATIONERS' HALL.

PREFACE.

" WHAT is there in a NAME?" asks the immortal Shakspeare. The Author of "The Modern Gilpin" would humbly respond,—A great deal in the present case: for if Cowper had not given his celebrated " Johnny Gilpin" to the world, the following *bagatelle*, in all probability, would never have been written; or if indeed it had, it would not have been published, wanting, as it then would have done, the powerful assistance of a celebrated " name." So much for the title; and now for the hero.

The character of "John Oldstock" (who, by-the-by, is a member of that noted fraternity, yclept " Marine Store Dealers,") affords a striking and incontrovertible evidence of the fact, that a man may follow

A 2

a low profession or calling, and be, not-
withstanding, a very worthy member of
society—nay, even a *gentleman,** in the *truest*
sense of the term.

Our hero, for the first time in his life,
finds himself on board a steamer, on a
bright autumnal morning—gradually relaxing
from the every-day concerns of a life of
business, and entering joyfully into the
heart-stirring scenes of bustle and activity.

The Author has endeavoured to sketch,
in the following pages, a faithful, though
vivid, outline of our noble *Thames*, with
its tributary streams; but, of course, such
a sketch only as the passing glance from
a steam-boat will permit.

* The meaning of this term is very equivocal. A
witness on a trial being questioned as to his reason
for supposing a certain person to be a gentleman,
replied, "Why, *he kept a horse and chaise!*" This
is settling the question of gentility with a vengeance.
Johnson, in his definition of the word, says nothing
about such a qualification as this.

THE MODERN GILPIN,

&c. &c.

"He little dreamt, when he set out,
Of running such a rig."

PART I.

JOHN OLDSTOCK was a store-keeper,
In far-fam'd Seven-Dials;
An ebon nymph grac'd his shop-door—
He dealt in rags and phials.

John was not young, nor was he old:
His years twice two-and-twenty;
His form was cast in roughest mould:
But good to all e'er meant he.

He was a sober, careful man,
　　And constant at his labour;
He'd seen fair days, ere foul began—
　　Was first to serve a neighbour.

His spouse was fair as spouse could be—
　　To Oldstock quite a treasure:
A prudent helpmate—wise as he—
　　But lov'd a little pleasure.

She lov'd a little gentle jaunt,
　　To Highgate or to Hampstead;
And sometimes visited an aunt,
　　Who liv'd quite snug at Flamstead.

While John, good soul, still plodded on;—
　　To pleasure's walks a stranger;
" There's nought to me like home," thought John;
　　" I ne'er shall be a ranger."

But men are wayward creatures, sure,
　　The best of them are fickle;
But time can resolution cure—
　　For time's the best of pickle,

So, as at supper sat the pair,
　　After the day's exertion,
Dame spoke so well—John told the fair,
　　He'd take a day's excursion.

And thus he thought, and thus he said,
　　" To-morrow we'll rise early;
And spend a day with Ann and Fred,
　　And Mister and Mistress Shirley.

" We've seen but nought of life you know;
　　For once we'll have a glimmer;
So, love, get ready—we will go
　　To Gravesend, by the steamer."

The dame return'd him many smiles—
　　For she did never grumble;
As ten was booming thro' Saint Giles',
　　They into bed did tumble.

PART II.

'Twas six o'clock (they rose at five)—
  The sun was up and bright'ning;
The parlour ready—friends arrive,
  The cat and kitten fright'ning.

For John, as soon as he awoke,
  Set off to fetch the party;
And when he'd found the street and folk,
  Invited them right hearty.

Few friends had John—but these were true,
  And merry ones beside:
For all his other *friends*—the crew—
  Had turn'd with fortune's tide.

Well, now at breakfast sit the lot,
  And joy beams round each feature;
They talk of Gravesend, and what not;
  And all are full of glee, sure.

And now the hour is drawing near—   .
  The time for them to sally;
The hamper fill'd with goodly cheer—
  No longer need they dally.

A coach is call'd—they mean to ride,
  And quickly all are seated,
Save John, who meant to sit outside,
  Lest he should be o'erheated.

Well, now the door is clos'd at last,
  Up bustles Mister Crottles;
The dealer cries, " Friend, not so fast !
  I want a few good bottles !"

John Oldstock was not pleas'd to find
  A hindrance to his jaunting;
But wisely thought he'd stay behind—
  In prudence seldom wanting.

Fain would his friends have stay'd for John,
  But this he'd not allow:
He told the coachman to drive on,
  And he would quickly follow.

PART III.

The business done—the dealer gone,
  John left the place *instanter*;
Though he was fat, and hot the morn,
  He set off in a canter.

He turn'd the corners one by one,
  For have a ride he would not:
He wisely argu'd, he could run
  Where cabs and 'busses could not.

Well, hat in hand, he trudges through
  Close streets, and lanes, and alleys;
At last the steam appears to view,
  And towards the quay he sallies.

Now safe on board, Oldstock looks out
  For friends—but they had started;
And swift the steamer tack'd about,
  And through the flood it darted.

The Custom-house then met his gaze,
   And now he views the Tower—
A fabric rear'd in by-gone days,
   To curb the City's power.

And now the vessel paddles through
   The floating forest's mazes:
Eight hundred sail, of every hue—
   With home and foreign faces.

At length the Captain's voice is heard,
   As from the bridge[1] he sees her
Flying along—he gives the word—
   The boy cries, "Stop her! ease her!"

Now through the Pool[2] she stately goes,
   And Limehouse Reach is neared;
Where round the Isle[3] the river flows,
   The horse-shoe form is cleared.

And Deptford town and Greenland docks,
   Add to the eye's confusion;
With churches and West India Docks,
   Warehouses in profusion.

The *Ravensbourne* here runs to seek
　　Its sire, with fond embraces :
Throws all its charms into the Creek,
　　And mingles all its graces.

PART IV.

The boat to Greenwich runs amain,
   And round the point is steered;
The band strikes up the well-known strain,
   To British hearts endeared.

When John beheld his native place,
   His heart with joy was swelling;
Bright thoughts pass'd through his mind apace-
   All sense of gloom dispelling.

" Lo ! there's the spot that gave me birth;
   And yon's the far-fam'd hill, [4]
Where lads and lasses roll in mirth,
   And romp with right good-will.

" And there's the princely pile of stone, [5]
   For British veterans reared,
Whose fiery ardour long has flown—
   By foes no longer feared !

" Ah ! generous spot ! I love thee still !
  Though forc'd from thee to sever ;
Thy noble Park, [6] with One-tree Hill, [7]
  Shall grace my memory ever."

And long he gaz'd, and thought withal
  Of childhood's days unclouded ;—
Meanwhile the steamer reach'd Blackwall,-
  East India Docks, so crowded.

And Woolwich Arsenal, I ween—
  Its town 'mid scenes inviting ;
And Bow Creek, too, may now be seen,
  The *Thames* and *Lea* uniting.

Now Shooter's-hill bursts o'er the sight,
  In native grandeur rising :
Here Health, and Peace, and Joy alight,—
  The city's walks despising.

And Barking Creek is distanc'd quite ;
  And Dagenham likewise ;
O'er land and wave the sun shone bright,—
  And great was John's surprise.

For he had rode but once before
    On London's flood so merry:
And then he cross'd from Kent's fair shore,
    To Limehouse, in a wherry.

Now marshes on each side appear;
    Swift are the paddles turned;
But soon a fairer scene is near,
    For Erith is discerned.

PART V.

Beneath the woody heights of Lesnes,
  Unite the *Cray* [8] and *Darent* [9]—
Give tribute to majestic *Thames*,
  And slumber with their parent.

Past Purfleet and each magazine
  The steamer now is gliding;
And Stone's neat village church is seen,
  While slowly runs the tide in.

And Greenhithe, too, in foliage drest;
  With Ingress Park uniting;
And Fidler's Reach, [10] and Thurrock West;
  And town of Grays inviting.

The pretty village of Northfleet
  Invites the eye's attention;
Here wildest Nature runs to greet
  The work of Art's invention. [11]

Oldstock ne'er thought he was so near
   To Gravesend's town, so noted,
As towards its light and handsome pier
   The merry vessel floated.

But who is yon fair, comely dame,
   Who on the pier is standing?—
She's just arrived in the " Fame"—
   Its passengers are landing.

She meets the astonish'd gaze of John,—
   Joy from each eye is flashing:
But, lo! the steamer still drives on,
   And past the place is dashing.

And then, too late, our hero saw
   That he had made a blunder;
And now the sun's bright beams withdraw,
   And loudly rolls the thunder.

Chang'd is the aspect of the scene—
   Dark, heavy clouds impending;
*The lightning's vivid flash is seen;
   The rain is fast descending.

Friend John was one who seldom sighed
    At actions past controlling;
Each frown of fate he still defied—
    Life's shadows backward rolling.

Some would have fum'd and made complaint,
    And wish'd them back in London;
This was *his* maxim—true, though quaint,—
    " What's done, cannot be undone."

PART VI.

It rain'd until the Fort,⁽¹²⁾ to view,
    A speck seem'd in the distance;
While swifter still the vessel flew,
    And brav'd the tide's resistance.

Securely shelter'd from the blast,
    Sly Mirth each head is ducking;—
Whilst Chalk, Higham, and Cliff, are pass'd;
    East Tilbury, too, and Mucking.

Yon heap likewise, o'er whose fair bow'rs
    Destruction long has hover'd:
Old Cowling Castle's time-worn tow'rs,
    With ivy richly cover'd.

But summer's stormy clouds will fade,
    When Sol peeps in the distance:
So in this world, 'mid light and shade,
    We pass our brief existence.

The rain is o'er—the deck is dried,
  By mop and heat together;
Below no longer folks abide—
  Each heart's light as a feather.

The dance begins—each beau and belle,
  Trip through the quadrille's figure;
The waltz, and country dance as well,
  Perform'd with graceful vigour.

The steam is up—with might and main,
  The vessel's making headway;
And as she turns the Isle of Graine,
  She's running towards the *Medway*.

Through the deep waters at the *Nore*—[13]
  Past Sheerness she is gliding:
Where, to defend each neighbouring shore,
  A warlike fleet is riding.

The Royal Dock and Forts are seen,
  In proud defiance standing;
And hills and dales in beauteous green,
  Attention due commanding.

Now music's soft and plaintive sounds,
    O'er *Medway's* stream is floating;—
And when 'tis past, John looks around—
    With joy each object noting.

On the right side of *Medway's* flood,
    Proud Upnor's pile appears,
Whose stanch old walls have long withstood
    The storms of by-gone years.

At length, her goal the steamer's near'd—
    Off Chatham she is lying;
And when alongside boats appear'd,
    Ashore the folks were hieing.

PART VII.

In Chatham town, at further end,
　　Where rising ground appears,
John knew an old and valu'd friend,
　　Whom he'd not seen for years.

For him John search'd, from street to lane-
　　His dwelling, too, inquired,
Of those he met, but could not gain
　　The answer he desir'd.

So he the hunt gave o'er, at last—
　　His steps quickly retracing;
But, lo !—as he the corner pass'd,
　　His friend ran up against him.

With sudden shock each bounded back
　　Full half a dozen feet;
But soon shook hands, with hearty smack,
　　So overjoy'd to meet.

Now, in the parlour of his friend,
   Our hero's smugly resting;
In converse they the moments spend—
   Old wine and friendship testing.

How brief is time! its months and years,
   With swiftness fly along;
But shorter still the time appears,
   When friends we are among.

Light pass the hours when old friends meet,
   After a lengthen'd period;
They're young again, and joy's complete—
   Ne'er with each other wearied.

But brightest joys will have an end—
   So frail are pleasure's wiles;
And John takes leave of his old friend
   With friendship's earnest smiles.

To gain his place, John quickly hied,
   And trudg'd along light-hearted;
But found, when at the river-side,
   The steamer had departed!

And far beyond he saw the smoke,
 In one black stream ascending;
In sober truth, it was no joke—
 His passage on't depending.

To hail the boat, he jump'd about
 With all his main and might,
He wav'd his hat, and loud did shout-
 But soon 'twas out of sight.

PART VIII.

ROMANTIC is fair Rochester,
  And every scene around;
With charms wild Nature's dress'd her—
  Each spot's enchanted ground.

Here *Medway's* noble stream runs by
  The Castle's proud remains,—
Whose huge and stanch old walls so high,
  Their giant strength retain.

With deep regret, but cheerful mood,
  This bright scene John's forsaking;
And cross'd the pretty bridge to Strood—
  The road to Gravesend taking.

The way was long, the day was bright;
  And John oft stopt to rest;
And long ere Gravesend was in sight,
  The sun was in the west.

B

But hope and perseverance will
   All obstacles surmount;
And he, at last, sees Windmill-hill, [14]
   Which cockneys love to mount.

He bustled quickly on the pier—
   No steamer could he see; ·
Said John, "I am too late, I fear"—
   And right enough was he.

Our hero, in a pensive mood,
   Now sallies up the High-street;
One moment at the top he stood—
   Then moved on towards Northfleet.

And as he thus is sauntering on,
   Each object new discerning;
An empty post-chaise wheels along,
   From Rochester returning.

The post-boy's arch, inviting glance
   Caught John's eye in a minute;
And to the chaise he did advance,
   And quickly he sprung in it.

Bang went the door—the post-boy's up—
　　The whip and spurs applying;
The wheels fly round—the dust flies up,
　　And John to town is hieing.

PART IX.

How sudden change from scene to scene,
 Plays tricks with fancy's flow—
Morn's brief events seem pass'd, I ween,
 A week or two ago.

But with our friend an age it seem'd,
 Since from his home he'd strayed;
Still o'er his features mildness beam'd—
 A well-form'd mind displayed.

Now as to Dartford he drew nigh,
 From window John was peeping;—
And then he yawn'd and rubb'd each eye-
 And soon was soundly sleeping.

But still the chaise kept rattling on,
 And only once it tarried;
Nor could the jolting wake friend John,
 Who swift towards London's carried.

But, as the shadows of the night,
 O'er hill and dale were frowning,
Oldstock awoke in sudden 'fright—
 He dreamt that he was drowning.

He bounded forward—bruis'd his nose,
 And loosen'd his front teeth;—
Just then the harvest moon arose,
 And pointed out Blackheath.

Swift roll'd the chaise to Lewisham,
 And cross'd the stream so bright, [15]
And quick to the Kent Road it ran,
 Where Oldstock did alight.

It struck eleven, when in the street,
 His shop-door John discerned;
And scarce within he'd plac'd his feet,
 Ere wife and friends returned.

Now Mistress Oldstock's deep regrets,
 With tears of joy are starting;
But cheer'd by John she soon forgets
 The length of such a parting.

" My dear," said Oldstock, " dry your eyes,
   How vain are these repinings !
And useless quite are tears and sighs—
   The spirits undermining.

" On me, you know, light falls the blow,
   Inflicted by a feather:
But, for your sake, when next we go,
   We'll e'en go all together."

————

THERE is on England's lofty throne
   A youthful, gentle creature;
The Graces claim her as their own,
   And beauteous is each feature.

May Heaven o'er fair VICTORIA smile,
   And e'er from harm defend her;
Long may she reign in Britain's Isle,
   And happiness attend her!

NOTES.

Note (1) page 11.

THE *bridge* is a temporary platform, placed across the deck, and supported by the paddle-boxes. It is erected for the convenience of the Captain, who, from his elevated position, can give the necessary orders with greater facility, in passing through the over-crowded Pool.

Note (2) page 11.

The limits of the Port of London reach from London-bridge to the North Foreland in Kent, and to the Naze in Essex; but the ships trading to London, usually moor from the bridge to *Limehouse*, in which space it is computed that about eight hundred sail can lie afloat, at the moorings, at low water. This space is called the *Pool*.

Note (3) page 11.

The *Isle of Dog or Dogs.* This curious bend in the river, which is of the form of a horse-shoe, took

its name, it is said, from the following circumstance :—
A murder having been committed on this spot, a faithful dog lingered near the body of his murdered master, and would not leave it, except, when compelled by hunger, he would swim over to Greenwich; and then as quickly return. This act being constantly repeated, was at last noticed by the watermen plying there; who, following the devoted animal, discovered the body of the murdered man. The remainder of the story is soon told. The dog returning to Greenwich shortly afterwards, on his usual errand, snarled at a waterman who sat there, and would not be beaten off. The waterman being apprehended, made a confession, and was executed on the spot. We do not learn what became of the dog.

Note (4) page 13.

On this hill may be seen the Royal Observatory, which stands on the site of a tower erected by the " good Duke of Gloucester."

Note (5) page 13.

The hospital for disabled seamen.

Note (6) page 14.

This park is, perhaps, one of the finest in England. It was laid out by Le Notre, in the time of Charles II., and is planted chiefly with elms and Spanish chestnuts. In this park are remains of various *ancient barrows*, most of which were opened in 1784, and found to contain, amongst other things, spear-heads, knives, lumps of iron, broad-headed nails, with decayed wood adhering to them, human bones and hair, and fragments of woollen cloth.

Note (7) page 14.

One-tree hill is distinguished by its height and its one solitary tree, which is firmly rooted in its brow. Few persons would be silly enough to run down this steep hill. A fool-hardy attempt of this kind was attended with loss of life some years ago.

Note (8) page 16.

The *Cray*, called by the Saxons *Crecca*, which signifies a rivulet, rises at Newell, in the parish of Orpington, flows almost due north, and giving name to St. Mary Cray, Paul's Cray, Foot's Cray, North Cray, and Crayford, winds to the north-east through Crayford marshes, joins the river Darent in Dartford creek, and falls with that river, in an united stream, into the Thames. This river is well stored with trout of excellent flavour, and more than ordinary size.

Note (9) page 16.

The *Darent* rises in the parish of Westerham, whence flowing north-east, it passes Valence, Brasted,

Sundrish, and Chipsted, to River-head, where directing its course nearly north, it runs by Otford, Newhouse, Shoreham, Eynsford, and Farningham, to South Darent. Hence winding. on north-westwardly to Dartford, it acquires the name of Dartford Creek, and enlarged by the Cray, as already mentioned, enters the Thames at Long Reach, being navigable as far as Dartford.

Note (10) page 16.

Probably called so, from the irregular swelling, or fiddling, as seamen call it, of the waters.

Note (11) page 16.

Here stands a castellated mansion, called Ormns, or the Orm, which has a very noble appearance.

Note (12) page 19.

Tilbury Fort,—which was originally built as a kind of block-house by Henry VIII., but converted into a regular fortification by Charles II. after the Dutch fleet had sailed up the river *Medway* in 1667, and burnt three English men-of-war at Chatham. Various additions have since been made, and the fort is now mounted with a great number of guns. Some traces of the camp which, in the time of Queen Elizabeth, was formed here to oppose the descent of the Spanish Armada, are still visible.

Note (13) page 20.

The *Nore* is an estuary, and is properly the water which runs between the Isles of Graine and Sheppy; here it is that the rivers *Thames* and *Medway* lose their names and are called the *Nore*.

Note (14) page 26.

Windmill-hill, in the vicinity of Gravesend, is the favourite resort of thousands of persons from the metropolis in the summer time.

Note (15) page 29.

The river *Ravensbourne*. This pretty little river rises on Keston Common, Kent; and directing its course between Hayes and Bromley, and being augmented by several rivulets, runs towards the pleasant village of Lewisham. After passing through other places, and receiving its silvery tribute from various rills, it finally falls into the Thames at Deptford Creek.

Crocker, Printer, 5, Garuaalt-place, Spa-fields, London.

JOHN CROCKER,

Working Account-Book Manufacturer and Station

5, Garnault-place, Spa-fields.

J. C. respectfully informs the inhabitants of Spa-fields and its Vicinit
that being a Manufacturer and Retailer he can afford to offer his goo
at the following prices:—

Tradesmens' Red Leather Books for families, lettered in gold at 6s. per doz

Ruled Books.	Pages.	s.	d.	
Cut Flush, 13 in. long by 4 in. wide, and 8 inches long by 6½ in. wide, } containing	96 ..	0	10	eac
Ditto,..............ditto,.............ditto..	192 ..	1	4	do
Ditto, bound in Forrel, ditto,...........ditto..	288 ..	2	6	do
Ditto,.....ditto,.....ditto,...........ditto..	480 ..	3	6	d.
Ditto,.....ditto, 16 in. long by 6½ wide and 13 long by 8 wide } ditto..	288 ..	4	6	do
Ditto,.....ditto,....ditto,...........ditto..	480 ..	7	0	do
Ditto,.....ditto,....ditto,...........ditto..	760 ..	11	0	do
Ditto,.....ditto,...ditto,...........ditto..	960 ..	13	6	do
Ledgers in Rough Calf, 13 in. long by 8 wide ditto..	288 ..	7	0	do
Ditto,.....ditto,.....ditto,...........ditto..	480 ..	10	0	do
Ditto,.....ditto,.....ditto,...........ditto..	760 ..	14	6	do.
Ditto,.....ditto,.....ditto,...........ditto..	960 ..	18	6	do.
Ditto,.....ditto, 15 in. long by 10 in wide ditto..	480 ..	18	0	do.
Ditto,.....ditto,.....ditto,...........ditto..	760 ..	24	0	do.
Ditto,.....ditto,.....ditto,...........ditto..	960 ..	30	0	do.
Ditto,.....ditto, 19 in. long by 12 in. wide ditto..	480 ..	30	0	do.
Ditto,.....ditto,.....ditto,...........ditto..	760 ..	40	0	do.
Ditto,.....ditto,.....ditto,...........ditto..	960 ..	52	6	do.
Pawnbroker's Account Books, 19 in. long by 8 in. wide } do...	570 ..	15	0	do.
Ditto,...........ditto,..........ditto....ditto..	760 ..	18	6	do.
Ditto,...........ditto,..........ditto....ditto..	960 ..	22	0	do.
Ditto,...........ditto,..........ditto....ditto..	1152 ..	28	0	do.
Ditto,...........ditto, 16 in. long by 6½ wide do...	288 ..	5	0	do.
Ditto,...........ditto,..........ditto....ditto..	480 ..	8	0	do.
Ditto,...........ditto,..........ditto....ditto..	570 ..	9	6	do.
Baker's Ledgers, 16 in. long by 6½ in. wide, & 13 in. long by 8 in. wide } do...	288 ..	5	0	do.
Ditto,..................ditto..........ditto..	480 ..	8	0	do.
Ditto,..................ditto..........ditto..	570 ..	9	6	do.
Ditto,........ 15 in. long by 10 in. wide ditto..	480 ..	18	0	do.
Ditto,..................ditto..........ditto..	760 ..	24	0	do.
Ditto,..................ditto..........ditto..	960 ..	30	0	do.

The above Books are bound with Improved Patent Backs.

Outside Post Paper .... 5s. 6d. and 9s. 0d. per Ream.
Outside Foolscap.............. 10 0 " 12 6 ditto.
Inside Foolscap .... 15 0 " 17 6 ditto.
Insides Post :....... 8s. 6s. 12s. 15 0 " 17 6 ditto.
Coloured and Printing Demys, Double Crown, Royal Hand, Small Hand,
and Brown Papers equally low.
Bag Cap Brown 6d., 8d., and 10d. per quire. Imperial Brown 1s.,
1s. 2d., 1s. 4d., and 1s. 6d. per quire.
Very large Brown for Woollen Drapers and Tailors at 2s. 6d. and 2s. 9d. per qr.

ALSO,

GENERAL NEWSPAPER AGENT.

WEEKLY and MONTHLY PUBLICATIONS REGULARLY SUPPLIED.

☞ *J. C. wishes to impress upon the minds of his friends, that the strictest punctuality may be depended upon in the delivery of orders for Daily and Weekly Newspapers.*